Tuning In

Six Ways to Reclaim Your Life from Technology

Adam McLane

Tuning In

Six Ways to Reclaim Your Life from Technology

By Adam McLane

Tuning In

Publisher: Mark Oestreicher
Managing Editor: Tamara Rice
Cover Design: Adam McLane
Layout: Adam McLane
Creative Director: Johnny Gutenberg

ISBN-13: 978-1-942145-32-5
ISBN-10: 1-942145-32-2

The Youth Cartel, LLC
www.theyouthcartel.com
Email: info@theyouthcartel.com
Born in San Diego
Printed in the U.S.A.

Contents

Introduction

When I turned 30, it was no big deal.

There was a big party in my backyard. It felt like I was being recognized by our society as an adult for the first time in my life. Though I'm not sure how being married with two kids, a mortgage, and a job serving as the youth pastor at a small church in the Detroit suburbs wasn't considered "adult" when I was in my 20s. But that's how turning 30 felt; I was publicly recognized for something I'd already been living.

When I turned 40, it was a big deal.

Only my closest friends and family even knew about my birthday. There was no party because I didn't want one. I've never been a fan of celebrating my own birthday, though I enjoy celebrating others. As such, I've long since hidden my birthday from Facebook. The birthday alert on Facebook is my least favorite feature. The very last thing I want on my birthday is the nagging task of "liking" people's Happy Birthday comments.

While turning 40 was no big deal externally, it was *kind of* a big deal to me *internally*. It pains me to admit it.

And while I didn't go out and buy a Corvette or experience a deep-seated midlife crisis, turning 40 has been majorly introspective.

- *What kind of husband am I, really?*
- *With a middle schooler and a high schooler in our house, how am I doing as a dad?*
- *Am I being faithful to my life's calling?*
- *Am I being faithful to my potential?*

More than 20 years ago, when I was a sophomore at Moody Bible Institute, a class full of 19-year-olds laughed when our Psychology 101 professor recalled what turning 40 felt like. He said, "One night you'll wake up in a cold sweat. You look around at your wife and children, you look at your career, you look at what you are doing with your life, you feel your fat belly, and you say to yourself: 'Is this it? Is this who I've become?'"

We laughed. I laughed. Midlife crisis? What a bunch of crap. But you know what? He was right.

I don't know if it was the physical age of 40 or just an awakening to my bad habits of a decade marked by hard work. All I know was the last year has been a series of crises and reorientations.

Tuning Out

This book is an outworking of that series of internal crises, mainly brought about by the ubiquitous reality of technology and social media. Over the past decade these technologies have fostered both good and bad habits. I have a feeling that these aren't just my own problems. I think we are each facing similar challenges as the very nature of work and home life shifts with the encroachment of technology that blurs the line more and more between between work, non-work, and what is even considered work.

For example, I found that I could get ahead of my piles of work if I worked when everyone else wasn't. So, I began seeing holidays, weekends, and nights as prime opportunities to do work. But that came at a high cost. Instead of affording myself that time with my family to rest, recuperate, and reorient (the very definition of recreation), I just doubled down on work and work and more work.

This pattern, which I once considered hustle, I now see as *being* hustled.

I had exchanged The Calling for *a* calling.

Here's what I mean: These work habits gave me permission to tune in to my career, gaining competitive

11

advantage at what I perceived as my vocational calling, by tuning out what I now recognize to be my *actual* calling as a husband, father, and neighbor.

The message of Cat Steven's "Cat's in the Cradle"—written long before the intrusions of Twitter, Facebook, and Instagram—isn't that tuning out what's really important is inevitable, rather, that it's preventable. So, the point of this short book is to explore the times and places where it's entirely necessary to tune out from work, technology, and social media.

Tuning In

Conversely, misguided priorities can't be resolved exclusively by tuning out, because tuning out of social media altogether is a Band-Aid to a larger problem, not a solution. Instead, we'll explore tuning in to content and movements that really matter in light of our personal values, to the exclusion of stuff that doesn't matter as much but might be noise or brain candy begging for a response.

For example, I found myself wasting a lot of time consuming news and then having raucous conversations online about it. Is that important? It can be. I've learned Facebook friends are far more malleable about what they consider firmly held positions than they let on. But is it my calling to argue someone away from a firmly held position on Facebook? Is that what I'm on this planet to do? No. So I needed to cut that back dramatically.

The smartphone is a powerful tool for feeding your brain's insatiable appetite for new information. But it's not human. It doesn't need your attention to the exclusion of the people you live with. Your smartphone couldn't care less if you read everything in your RSS reader, check every email message, respond to every comment on Facebook, or even read every text message.

But your kids do. Your coworkers do. Your spouse does. The people you're having dinner with certainly do. The more I've intentionally owned my smartphone, the better things have gotten for me.

The result of this commitment? I've been able to better tune in to things that really matter to me. My family. My home. My community.

In the following pages, you'll discover a series of essays which deal with everyday challenges you and I face as a direct result of technology. I believe that most of these challenges and bad habits creeping into our daily lives are happening because none of us made a careful and conscious decision to allow technology in. Instead, things like smartphones and social media have crept into our daily routines out of convenience or fascination or some other cultural force.

In each essay, you'll see a repeated theme: As you tune things out that aren't important, you'll have better focus and more energy for tuning in to things that are really important to you.

The goal isn't guilt, it's action.

I believe each of our personal callings in life are far too important to waste our lives tuning in to the wrong things.

Tuning In Principle:

Tune in to what matters most.

CHAPTER 1
The Most Popular Blog in the World... For a Day

"There's a bar at the top of this mountain, right?"

"Yep. Cold beer and an amazing view. You'll love it."

"Good, because I hate the going-up part of climbing a mountain. You've got me on some sort of death march. I'm convinced you're trying to kill me."

"I know. You always whine when we hike up things. It'll be worth it."

She was lying to me. I knew it.

Actually, she wasn't lying to me.

I knew all along there wasn't cold beer at the top of the mountain. It wasn't even really much of a mountain, more like a large hill. Yet for someone like me, who likes the idea of hiking but not its realities, this ascent might as well have been Mount Everest—2,500 feet of elevation change from the roadside trailhead to the summit felt like 29,000. "Where is my oxygen mask? Where is Sir Edmund Hillary's body?" (Fact check: Hillary didn't die on Mt. Everest.)

Of course, there wasn't a bar at the top to sit at and enjoy the view. In fact, I'd invented the whole notion of a bar as a way to motivate myself to keep going. At the top was only a big rock and a stellar view of Joshua Tree National Park in California's Mojave Desert.

This crisp December morning Kristen beamed with enthusiasm. She comes alive in the outdoors. Hiking to a beautiful vista is her happy place. She was full of energy and excited to get to the top. I was faking it badly. I wanted to like it for her sake, but was just too out of shape to find it enjoyable.

As we reached the summit of this small hill of a mountain it was clear this was a place we should take a selfie. In fact, every fellow hiker was taking selfies. We each pulled out our smartphones to snap pictures.

On the ascent, there hadn't been cell coverage, but at the summit there was a sliver of 4G. So, while Kristen began taking pictures of the scenery, I refreshed my email and opened up Facebook out of habit.

Nothing happened. Just a spinning wheel. So, I joined her in taking pictures.

We'd scheduled this getaway to Joshua Tree to reconnect and relax, to spend time alone without our children, to celebrate a great year and get ready for another. We'd spent the night at a small cabin 25 miles into the desert, past Nowhere, California. We'd stayed up late, stared at the stars only a lightless desert sky provides, shot gorgeous time-lapse video, and did what we always do when we visit places: talk about what it would be like to live there.

We didn't really want to live in the desert. But a small vacation cottage we could list on Airbnb? Maybe.

Our life was going a million miles an hour. Our kids were growing up quickly, our thirties melting away like butter in the microwave, and it seemed as if 2013 had been a blur of bills and work and weekends. But this short trip was what we needed, a deep breath at the end of one year to prepare for the next.

I was happy at the top of the mountain. So happy. Everything felt carefree. I felt a tiny bit of accomplish-ment for reaching the summit, which helped me forget the difficulty of getting there. Kristen was, of course, right. The view was worth it. I'm glad she dragged me up the hill. It was beautiful. The breeze, the fresh air, the horizon before us.

When we spend time alone together exploring nature, my mind races through all of the adventures we've had as a couple. We met when we were only 18 years old, and in so many ways we've grown up together—our entire adult experience is intertwined together. This adventure in Joshua Tree joined a long list of firsts in life we've experienced together.

On the top of that mountain, snapping selfies, we were 22 again.

We lingered. We sat in silence. We stared across the valley floor to the next peak. Unrushed, we took it in, holding on to the moment. Maybe it was an hour? Maybe it was 15 minutes. It felt good.

Before the tug of reality came. It was time to go.

It was December 28th, 2013. Little did I know that this moment was the pivot point for the next year.

When we couldn't post the selfies to Instagram because of the poor reception, we started back down the trail to our car. It wouldn't refresh or pull in anything new. So, I just stuck it back in my pocket and tried to forget about it.[1]

As we rounded the first set of switchbacks I noticed the phone in my pocket was hot. Like, really hot. It was so hot it felt like it was burning my thigh. I stopped on the trail, took my phone out, and tried to figure out what was going on. I slid my finger across the screen to unlock it and stood in amazement. The limited coverage meant that my phone had continued to try to connect to email and text and Facebook and Twitter even though I had put it away. And once it found a strong signal, so much data came at once that it overheated the processor, almost literally burning up my phone.

Text messages from friends were rolling in, notifications from Twitter and Facebook filled the screen, and my inbox was downloading hundreds and hundreds of new messages. Everything was coming in at once, piling on top of everything else.

My mind raced. What in the world is going on? Why was this happening?

I checked Facebook and quickly found out. A blog post I had written four months prior to this, in August 2013, called "Why You Should Delete Snapchat" had been shared on Facebook 100,000 times before lunch. Friends, some of whom I'd not heard from since high school, were messaging me: "I'm seeing this post everywhere. It's taken over my Facebook timeline. Did you write this?" Huge threads of comments had emerged on the blog post. I opened up Twitter and there were hundreds of mentions and seemingly unending discussion about what I'd written.

My head spun.

"What's the matter? Is everything OK?"

"Yeah, a blog post blew up. Tons of traffic. It's crazy." I didn't yet have words to describe what I'd just seen. "Whatever, let's get to the car."

In an instant I went from a serene, holy moment of connection with my wife to emotional chaos—my mind racing 10,000 miles per hour about something I'd written four months prior.

I tried pushing it away. "I'll deal with it later, when we get home."

But the moment was over. The joy I'd felt was gone. Even as I tried to put my phone away it was impossible to unsee what I'd seen.

22

On the drive home I tried to not think about it. We stopped for a date shake at a Southern California desert tourist trap. It was fun, but I kept catching myself refreshing my stats on the WordPress app: 200,000 visitors. Refresh: 220,000 visitors. *Wait, what does that comment say?* Refresh: 280,000 visitors. Texts from friends congratulating me. Messages from people I barely knew asking me how I was doing this. Emails from radio and television booking people wanting me on their shows. Refresh: 450,000 visitors.

Lord, have mercy. Let me just enjoy the rest of this day away with Kristen. We need this. I need this.

"It's crazy." That's all I kept saying and thinking. It was crazy. It made no sense why something I'd written so long ago would now take off. I had no frame of reference to grasp onto.

I kept thinking, *I don't need this.* In fairness, for the last 10 years as a blogger I'd wanted this. In a sense, I'd been working towards something like this happening. I wanted it to happen, I really did. My biggest day ever had been 30,000 visitors. But now? I was getting 30,000 visitors every time I refreshed the app, and it didn't feel at all how I'd thought it would.

I don't even remember the two-hour drive home. I

wanted to forget about what was happening. I wanted to push it out of my mind and go back to the top of the mountain. I wanted to feel the joy again. I wanted to take in every precious second of alone time with Kristen.

But it was gone.

We got home, unloaded the car, the kids and my in-laws welcomed us wanting to hear about our trip and share the details of all the stuff they did while we were gone. And I just drifted off to my desk, opened up my laptop, and started working.

By the end of the day my blog, which averages about 1,000 daily visitors, saw *1.2 million unique visitors.* More than 300,000 people shared my post on Facebook in 15 hours. Most of the evening I just stared at Google Analytics live stats, which showed 3,000 to 4,000 people across the world reading my post at the same time.

As a blogger, it was mind-blowing.

I was in the midst of living the blogging dream and by every measure of the online life, this was a huge success. It felt big because it was big. In a lot of ways it changed everything.

When you hear about something *going viral* you don't really think about how it happens. For me, it happened when I wasn't even paying attention. It happened when I had absolutely nothing to do with it. I wasn't the cause. In the end, it happened because news broke about a group of hackers exploiting the sophomoric coding of early versions of Snapchat. The app was so unsecure that the usernames and passwords needed to access their database were stored in the app itself. The key to accessing millions of users' personal information was available to anyone who downloaded the app for free and opened it in free software provided by Apple to developers. So, when a hacker published the usernames, emails, and passwords of a few million users online, so-called "mommy bloggers" started sharing my post about the dangers of Snapchat. Everything early users thought about Snapchat was actually a lie. It wasn't anonymous, and the images they'd been told would disappear didn't.

I didn't make my blog post go viral from some brilliant marketing scheme or campaign at all. I was just enjoying the desert with my wife. Instead, my blog went viral because a few female bloggers with large audiences issued a warning to fellow parents about Snapchat with an article I'd written not for mass appeal but to answer a question some parents had at a social media seminar earlier in 2013.

At the end of December 28th, 2013, my little blog, adammclane.com, was the #56 website in the world (#57 was *The New York Times*). For one day, in late 2013, I had the most popular blog in the world.

When Success Doesn't Feel Like It

I have a confession to make. December 28th, 2013, wasn't supposed to be about me. It was supposed to be about Kristen. So, something that everyone in my life thought was a massive success was actually a failure in my eyes.

We have a misshapen, ill-conceived, immature, and skewed view of what real-time success is.

Social media fosters the idea that we need a platform, something sharable like a TED Talk; a national or international seminal moment of going viral is the only validating metric of success. Careers are made because of these moments. In 2014, as a result of my blog post going viral, I spoke at dozens of schools and churches and community groups. I was most often introduced like this, "This is Adam McLane. His blog post about Snapchat has been read by millions of people, catapulting his blog to the number one blog in the world."

I'm here to tell you going viral is not success. It's a terrible goal. Ultimately going viral is an infection that leaves scars. Yes, I bear more scars from the experience than anything else.

Think about it. Who wants a virus or signs up for scars? Only someone who has never experienced the illness. Who calls having a virus a success? No one. The opposite is actually true. Sickness is destruction in the body at a cellular level that—if not stopped or reversed—can eventually lead to total bodily *failure*: death.

Success in the Kingdom isn't found on a platform. Jesus never called us to desire a platform. None of that platform success matters if your personal, private life— the inner workings of your soul—are not healthy. But the Christian life brings dead things to life.

Every time I see someone who thinks having a platform is the definition of success as a Christian leader I think about John 6.

Jesus had platform, baby. In an age when religious zealots were the first century version of reality TV shows, Jesus' miracles started pulling in crowds unlike anything else. Jesus was drawing crowds so large that he had to go up on top of hills or push out on the water in boats so that the acoustics would carry his voice for all to hear.

At a certain point it started to reach a pinnacle. You can imagine the disciples were talking amongst themselves: "This is amazing. We're a bunch of nobodies and this guy Jesus is the most popular person in Judea. He's going to bring about the Kingdom of God right now in front of our eyes and we're on his team? The whole world is going to know about us because of him!"

But Jesus wasn't about building his platform. He didn't look at what was happening and say, "Let's go bigger! Let's maximize. Let's blow this puppy up and reach millions." Instead, he did the opposite. He stood up and told the crowd to reconsider following him:

> *Jesus said to them, 'Very truly I tell you, unless you eat the flesh of the Son of Man and drink his blood, you have no life in you. Whoever eats my flesh and drinks my blood has eternal life, and I will raise them up at the last day. For my flesh is real food and my blood is real drink. Whoever eats my flesh and drinks my blood remains in me, and I in them. Just as the living Father sent me and I live because of the Father, so the one who feeds on me will live because of me. This is the bread that came down from heaven. Your ances-*

tors ate manna and died, but whoever feeds on this bread will live forever.' He said this while teaching in the synagogue in Capernaum.
                                    – John 6:53-59

You don't need a degree in political science to know that this wasn't a platform-building message. Standing in front of a crowd and inviting them to eat your flesh and drink your blood went over about as well in a platform-building way for Jesus as it would for you.

In fact, John 6:66 says, *"From this time many of his disciples turned back and no longer followed him."*

You see, according to Jesus, the Christian life isn't about platform building.

Instead, Jesus invites us to take up the cross and die with him. Success in the Kingdom is oftentimes tiny... When we allow our baptismal waters to penetrate the deep cracks of our soul's unforgiveness to bring grace, forgiveness, and renewal to our most private, hidden places, the dead parts of our lives spring to life like seeds stored through winter. In the Kingdom economy, we aren't accountable for a national influence. But we are accountable for an ordinary, local one. The Greatest Commandment of Jesus isn't to love our Twitter followers as ourselves. It's to love our neighbors as *ourselves*. What are we doing to allow the Good News of Jesus to impact *our own lives*? What about our loved ones? Our respective spouses and children? What about our neighbors and coworkers?

Ultimately, I believe seeking platform is failure. The platform isn't sinful in and of itself, but the seeking of it can certainly be. Instead of a platform, Jesus invites us to take up something far greater, the cross, to die to our society's desire for the platform and follow him, wherever that may lead.

This is our journey together. If you want a book about building up your influence in a social media-laden world, this isn't it. I can't help you. I'd rather eat that book than write that one.

Instead I want to invite you on a journey where together we will struggle to thrive in a 24/7/365 social media-driven world by opting in instead of opting out. I've found that it isn't about being bigger than you are. Trust me, you will kill your soul by propping yourself up as something you are not, can't possibly control, and are not accountable for fostering.

Thriving in today's world is ultimately about making your *you*, the secret/private self, smaller and smaller, more humble, and accessible to the people you are actually held accountable by God to love.

Jesus said, "I have come that you may have life, and have it to the full."

I want that. You want that. Let's find that together.

Tuning In Principle:

Tune in to the incarnation.

CHAPTER 2
Social Media Engagement as a Spiritual Discipline

In fifth grade, my dad married a woman who was Presbyterian, and I started going to church on a regular basis for the first time. He lived in Mishawaka, Indiana, and during the week I lived with my mom about 10 miles away in Granger. By chance, or as Presbyterians might call it, *providence*, a classmate of mine from school also went to the same church.

This means on day one I had a church buddy. I quickly learned that it was boring to sit with my parents but kind of fun to sit in the back and goof off with Cory. *That lasted exactly two weeks.* On the third Sunday I attended church, most likely to keep us quiet during the pastor's sermon, Cory and I were given a job. We were put in charge of the sound system. We were told how important it was to record the church service on cassette so that the shut-ins could hear the sermon later. I didn't know what a shut-in was. I didn't even really understand what a sound system was. But I liked having something to do that was more fun than sitting on my hands next to my dad. And we learned pretty quickly that if we got there early enough, one of the ushers would let us pull on the rope to ring the church bell. For a couple of 11-year-olds, we might as well have been elected kings of the church. We were hooked.

I didn't know much about Jesus but, to me, church was a place where I belonged. Each week I had a place to sit next to the sound board and after 30 minutes, the tape would loudly stop, I'd hit eject, and flip the cassette over and press record. Sometimes during the service the pastor would eyeball us, flashing us an up or down hand signal to indicate that we needed to turn the volume up or down. And, because we were two easily amused 11-year-olds, sometimes we'd crank it up real loud on purpose to make the microphone screech—you know, just to make sure the old ladies knew we were really running things up in the balcony.

Clearly Cory and I exhibited church leadership potential, right?

Flash forward to 11th grade. My mom married a man in the Army and we moved from Granger, Indiana to Germany. I'd never changed schools before much less been to another country, so this was a major change.

I also lost my place of belonging at my small Presby-terian church and was left searching for... *just about everything*. This move rattled me. I didn't have any friends, didn't fit in at my Department of Defense-run high school, didn't know what activities to join... Everything in my life felt up for grabs.

Into that loneliness stepped a missionary couple, Dan and Barb Evans. They were youth workers serving through the chaplaincy program to minister to the needs of teenagers. So, when they sat down at my table during lunch a few weeks after my arrival in Hanau, I was drawn to them. First, it struck me that a couple of adults who didn't work at the school voluntarily sat with us and seemed to really enjoy being there. Second, it seemed like they really cared. They weren't just there to promote something or sell or preach. They actually listened when you said something. And third, they were offering something that sounded fun and wasn't about drinking. (I'd had enough to drink in ninth and tenth grade, thank you very much.)

My relationship with Jesus took off as I started attending their youth group. Sometimes, usually when we were driving somewhere, Dan asked me real-life questions. He talked to me like an adult. And he wasn't afraid to prod or get personal or push past my Sunday-school answers. Over time, the more I got to know Dan

the more I wanted to know Jesus, which spun my life
into a whole new direction of intense Bible study and a
desire to minister to teenagers myself.

I share all of this because I kind of grew up *around*
church, but I didn't grow up in the church. I wasn't a
church kid. Since I wasn't acculturated from birth, I
have always had a lot of questions about things.

In fact, I believe one of my greatest assets to this day
is that I don't see church, evangelicalism specifically,
from the perspective of a native. Because I didn't grow
up in church, some things that we do at church still
don't make sense to me.

Retreating is great. Retreatism is bad.

Retreatism is one of those things that's never made
sense to me.

As we've seen social media become normative in our
society I've grown increasingly frustrated with a single
response to the challenges social media presents us with
as believers:

> Don't like what people are saying? Retreat.
> Don't like the people who are saying it? Retreat.
> Don't like the distraction? Retreat.

Don't like people having a voice? Retreat.
Don't like your staff having opinions? Retreat.
Don't like your students looking at their phones?
　　Retreat.
Don't like something you see online? Retreat.
Don't like the way you feel when you engage with
　　social media? Retreat.

Don't get me wrong. I understand that retreat is a legitimate spiritual discipline. Many of the great moments
in my own walk with Jesus have come as the result of
personal or group retreat. As a youth worker, I know the
power of retreat in helping young people connect with
Jesus in ways they struggle to in their daily lives.

But retreatism is bad because the dominant narrative
in the church, specifically as it relates to the 24/7/365
access that social media affords us, is rarely to practice
retreat (healthy) but instead retreatism (unhealthy).

Whether I'm listening to a sermon, reading a blog from
a favorite author, reading a book, or even attending a
scholarly conference from a Christian perspective, the
church seems to provide a single solution to dealing
with new realities of technology: retreat. You've
probably heard some version of it before: *The world
wears you down. Reconnect with Jesus by shutting
down, turning off, tuning out, getting away.*

In the fall of 2015, an experience at a conference brought this retreatism to a head for me. The topic was on technology as it relates to education and youth ministry. The first half of seminar after seminar would be great. The presenter would have an interesting premise, he or she would present primary research (or commentary on new research) that I hadn't seen or heard before. But in each session there would be a shift when it came to what we do with technology, particularly social media: retreat. For every problem presented, for every challenge, for every new opportunity the answer was always to step away, to pull away, to reconnect with Jesus by leaving social media behind. This was bothersome to me, because it's completely counter to my own experiences with social media.

Surely, I thought, there were Christian people out there who didn't look at social media as some sort of vice or a problem to be solved?

But no. Apparently for Christians the answer to all conflicts or temptations brought on by social media is singular: some variety of retreatism, withdrawal, or abstention.

Is this really it? Is retreat the only viable solution? Does engaging with the world drain you emotionally and spiritually while retreating fills you back up? Or is there another way? Are there alternative practices by other Christians who see it differently?

While I'd had this lingering feeling this was the predominant view of technology and social media among Christians, it was this experience at a conference that cemented my own desire to look for a well-formulated alternative narrative. So, I've spent the past year searching and experimenting to find some things that really work.

Let's review how we got here.

The Typical Response to Technology

The 15th-century invention of the printing press freaked out the established church. With Steve Jobs-like vision Johannes Gutenberg said,

> *Yes, it is a press, certainly, but a press from which shall flow in inexhaustible streams, the most abundant and most marvelous liquor that has ever flowed to relieve the thirst of men! Through it, God will spread his Word. A spring of truth shall flow from it: like a new star it shall scatter the darkness of ignorance, and cause a light heretofore unknown to shine amongst men.[2]*

41

Yet the church didn't embrace it as an opportunity to spread the gospel. To the religious establishment, the printing press was a threat. Remember this was centuries before the French and American Revolutions introduced free speech as basic human rights to the general public.

A century before Gutenberg, the church pushed back on Wycliffe's idea that people should hear the Bible in their own native language by declaring him a heretic. His ideas were dangerous and were effectively squelched after his death.

So when the printing press came along in the 15th century, with the possibility now that *anyone* could potentially share their own ideas with the masses or the possibility that *anyone* could now own their own Bible, reading it for themselves in the privacy of their home without the watchful interpretative eye of clergy. Well, this was a threat to their authority. The church saw itself as the ultimate messenger of truth and ideas in society, and therefore fostered a distrust of the printing press and its powers. To them the technology was dangerous.

There are lots of examples of this. Most famously with Martin Luther himself. Luther's writings, particularly his tracts written in response to what he felt were offenses committed by the institutional church, were not altogether different from the online statements of a person today who fact checks a sermon in real time, sharing inaccuracies or questioning the authority of the preacher on Twitter as the pastor preaches his sermon. Is this a rebellious act? It is certainly taboo. Most would consider this disrespectful. But is it morally wrong if it reveals truth? *Most people don't think so.*

Similarly, the church's effort to undercut the popular appeal of Luther's writings merely furthered his message and galvanized his authority amongst those who were fed up with the status quo for a wide variety of reasons. His growing popularity gave voice and credence to thoughts many held privately but had no way to express. When more and more people embraced his way of thinking and distrust of the established church grew—to oversimplify a lot of church history—the movement resulted in a brand new hybrid religion we now call Protestantism. Without the technology of the printing press we might not have Protestantism.

I would argue that social media is as revolutionary as the invention of the printing press. Though the printing press opened up new ideas to the masses without interference of the church or state, there was still a high cost to be paid in the equipment and distribution of these ideas. And today? Anyone in the world with a cheap smartphone and access to the internet can share their ideas. The printing press brought expression out of the realm of the elite, but social media brings expression to the street. Similar to the 15th century, as social media unleashes newfound expressive freedoms for billions of people, what new expression of Christianity might emerge? And how might the institutional church respond?

Will they respond the way they always have? Or will they reject the priesthood of the staff for the priesthood of all believers? Unfortunately, up to this point, all indications point to the former.

How did the church get locked into a single response to technology?

Luther didn't provide an altogether clean slate, *tabula rasa*, for Christianity. He carried on his own monastic tradition as a friar—a member of the Augustinian life he chose regulated by the Rule of Saint Augustine.[3] As such, Luther practiced spiritual disciplines which became codified in Protestant life and remain normative to most Protestants today:

> Retreat
> Fasting
> Solitude
> Contemplation

Isolation

In relation to technology, we carried forward some of the attitudes about society from the pre-Reformation days.

- During that time, "the world" was considered bad, evil at its core, to be engaged with but lived separately from, so as not to be caught up in sin.

- The Reformation, particularly the Puritan movement, heavily influenced European culture in efforts to reform society, not just religiously but also in fostering a desire to cleanse culture of sin. (See *The Scarlet Letter*.)

- Church culture's view on entertainment and media today is not altogether different than it was in the 15th and 16th centuries.

- "Secular" art is demarcated from "sacred" art. (Up until the early 2000s there was a distinct line between "secular" music/culture and "sacred" music/culture in the evangelical world.)

As it relates to social media, this historic distrust fed directly into the dystopian narrative that media is "engaging with the world"—a response not altogether different from the Reformers teaching congregants to distrust the theater since it might foster secular ideas in an otherwise "pure" culture.

As a result of all of this, our modern pastoral response is to teach congregants to use social media in small doses, to regularly withdraw, to fast, to separate from "the world" as a means of reconnecting with Jesus. And, as we'll discuss in future parts of this book, these are good practices. My argument is just that these are not the only responses the church should be teaching. Our response to "the world" is also fundamentally limited when we embrace this dystopian view and teach that technology and social media are dangerous. We must be challenged to reach beyond, to show that we can connect with Jesus anywhere we go.

I push back against the simplistic, binary teaching that we are to be "in the world but not of the world" to the exclusion of Jesus' incarnation, who—though he was God—took on human flesh to dwell among the world.

> *The Word became flesh and blood,*
> *and moved into the neighborhood.*
> – John 1:14a (The Message)

Let's Consider Adding an Atypical Response

I'd like to propose an incarnational response to living in a 24/7/365 world with social media. This response takes into account that Luther's religious order, the Augustinians, existed alongside different monastic orders that had *other* ways of viewing religious life. His religious order—along with the Benedictines, Dominicans, and Franciscans—largely withdrew from society. Some had monasteries that were completely separate from the population while others were in major cities. Some included vows which compelled adherents to dip their toes in "the world" *but they largely lived apart from common people.*

And yet, for centuries other orders, like the Society of Jesus (Jesuits), Congregation of Christian Brother-hood, and other institutions within Catholicism have *intentionally engaged and served the world as the hands and feet of Jesus.*

These groups don't see engaging with the world as a drain on their connection to Jesus, they see it as a way to tap into connecting with Jesus.

What if, instead of the default view that withdrawal from technology and social media is the best way to connect with Jesus, we embraced an alternative and likewise historically valid view that connecting with others via technology like social media is a legitimate way to connect with Jesus in his ministry among a dead and dying world? What if connecting with people on social media, dwelling among them, was seen as an expression of the gospel in our daily lives?

What if, in our daily lives, we practiced the Ignatius Examen as a way to intentionally engage the world around us—whether that's online on Snapchat or asking our neighbor how they're doing?

Tuning in to the World Around Us

In a post-Christian world, the line between the sacred and secular culture is blurred. Churches borrow seamlessly from "the world" just like "the world" borrows from the church. I have observed the very best churches often use and mimic marketing and entertainment from the secular world. And likewise, the very best businesses often create a culture that mimics the New Testament church.

Whether it's in an online Facebook group or a face-to-face meeting with people in my neighborhood, I find that people are not uninterested in Christianity or incurious about Jesus. What they want to know and what they need to see is that Jesus is Good News for them.

Too often what non-church people see online is church leaders who are wholly focused on the four walls of their church and programs to the exclusion of what's

Ignatius Examen

Engaging a Digital World

Over last few years I've shifted my focus from the spiritual discipline I grew up with, primarily focused on daily Bible reading and prayer, to embrace the Ignatius Examen. Several times a day I intentionally make time to reflect on these things.[4]

1. Thankfulness. Everything is a gift from God. What have I got to be grateful for today? How much do I take for granted? What has made me ungrateful, dissatisfied, frustrated? How have I been generous today?

2. Prayer for Light. I need to have my eyes opened: I need grace to see whether my gratitude is in proportion to the worth of the gifts of the Holy Spirit.

3. Examination. Review the events of the day. Look for God's presence in it. How was I drawn to God today? Have I been a sign of God's presence and love to the people I met today? Did I go out to the lonely, the sorrowful, the discouraged, the needy?

4. Sorrow. Face up to shortcomings. A true awareness of my sinfulness is still a gift granted in love by the Father, the Son and the Holy Spirit. I can express sorrow for the ways in which I have failed to respond to his love at work in me.

5. Looking to What's Next. Where do I need God's help? How will I face the next few hours?

6. Honest Online Engagement. While this is not traditionally part of the Ignatius Examen, of course, living the Christian life through honest engagement with my neighbors and friends on social media is an effective means of Christian witness in a society offended by formal evangelistic efforts.

going on in the larger community they so earnestly pray to serve.

Even as I type these words our society is reeling from another unarmed African American man being shot by police under suspicious circumstances. A look at the trending hashtags on Twitter shows what's really going on in our society. And yet this week most youth ministry leaders will relentlessly promote their programs, which (rest assured) will not address what everyone else seems to be talking about. Sadly, too many seem more infatuated with marketing our programs than reaching out.

Is the way you live Good News in the Neighborhood?

Several years ago I was serving as a youth pastor at a small Baptist church in the Detroit suburbs. By any standard measure things were going pretty well. Our church was growing. The teenagers in my ministry were growing spiritually. My children were growing up. And we were new owners of an old Victorian house.

When we moved in I made an effort to get to know every person whose property touched ours. Because of the weird shape of our lot, our house touched a lot of backyards. Over the first few months I found it easy to say hello and exchange pleasantries with all of our neighbors, so we knew a little about them and likewise. But there was one neighbor who dodged me. Sure, he'd give us the neighbor wave, but when I was in the backyard he made sure he was in the house. This had gotten beyond something coincidental; it was clear he didn't want to meet me, which made me want to meet him even more.

One day, I was out in the yard mowing grass, and he was in his backyard doing something too. I pushed my mower over towards where he was and made it seem like I'd run out of gas. (A minor pastoral lie for the sake of evangelism is OK, right?) As the mower engine turned off, I quickly took off my work gloves and stuck my hand across the fence. "Hi! I'm Adam. Nice to finally meet you."

"Hello, I'm Tom. Nice to meet you too… neighbor."

"I've seen you from time to time, but I guess it's just never worked out to say hello. I like your boat. Do you guys like to ski?"

We made small talk for a few minutes about his boat and the conversation drifted to talking about kids and sports and finally the weather.

Then Tom said, "Hey, I've been meaning to ask you.

What do you do for a living?"

Trust me, every ounce of my Evangelism Explosion training exploded in my cerebral cortex as he said those words. Oh baby, I was going to lead this guy to Jesus Greg Stier-style, and we'd have a brand new family in the church in a couple of weeks. *Yes!*

"I'm the youth pastor over at the Baptist church on 32 Mile Road. Do you know where that's at?"

"Ah, I see."

There was an awkward pause. I was kind of hoping he'd say more, so then I could somehow link in Romans 3:23.

He said, "I guess that makes sense. You seem really busy. You've got this big, beautiful yard. It's really one of the biggest backyards in town. And your kids play back here all the time. It seems to me that the only time I see you back here is to either mow the grass or host some kind of a party. See, I'm on disability, so I'm home all the time and I notice stuff. You leave early in the morning and you come home late. When you do come home you've always got visitors in your house or there's always something going on. Yeah, I know where your church is. But if that's how you're supposed to

52

live when you go to that church, I wouldn't ever want to have anything to do with it."

D. James Kennedy didn't write an answer for me to memorize on that one. Game. Set. Match.

"Wow. You've given me something to think about, Tom. It was really nice meeting you finally. I better get back to mowing."

Embarrassed and exposed, I got back to mowing.

That conversation across the fence 10 years ago changed everything for me. It helped me realize that in a post-Christian society *how I lived* was more important than merely what I believed or the words that came out of my mouth. Tom was absolutely correct. I was so busy being a pastor that I'd forgotten to be a fully present dad with my own kids. I was so engaged in what I was doing at the church that I was completely disengaged in any meaningful way with people I so desperately wanted to reach.

My ministry was going well, but I was failing and I didn't even know it.

As you and I engage on social media and, in my case, in my literal backyard, the question each of us faces, whether we're on staff at a church (or, like me, just a dad with a job) is, "Are we living in a way that's obviously Good News to the people around us?"

Are we tuning in? Or are we tuning out?

Tuning In Principle:
Tune in to re-creation.

CHAPTER 3

Remember the Sabbath, Keep It Holy

Why are we "just kidding" about one of the Ten Commandments?

It's not like Jesus offers a free pass on coveting your neighbor's wife.

It's not OK to kill someone or steal from your neighbor if you're really busy.

Committing adultery or dishonoring your parents—both still no-nos, right?

So, why do we give everyone a free pass about the Sabbath?

I don't like to blame things on church staff. But Sabbath is one of those things I think that most pastors have exchanged for convenience. They fill their Sundays up because for them it's a workday. It's the culmination of their work week. When I ask my friends in youth ministry if they regularly Sabbath, most will say they don't.

While we would all agree that Sabbath, for New Testament believers, is more a principle than a specific day, most can't even tell me the day that they would call their Sabbath day.

So, let's call a time out to act like a Baptist preacher for a minute and review the Fifth Commandment in three parts.

REMEMBER...

The term *remember* is a favorite refrain in the law. The heart of it is to push past pure religious observation and reflect on why this is a command. Remember, it starts in Genesis. On the seventh day God rested.

> *Thus the heavens and the earth were completed in all their vast array. By the seventh day God had finished the work he had been doing; so on the seventh day he rested from all his work. Then God blessed the seventh day and made it holy, because on it he rested from all the work of creating that he had done.*
>
> *– Genesis 2:1-3*

Was he tired? Of course not. An omnipotent God cannot tire. He didn't need a break, he chose to take one. Our tireless Creator made a day for the purpose of rest.

The word *remember* appears in the Old Testament almost 180 times in the New International Version. And the idea of remembering the Sabbath is a big deal to the Creator. God says *remember* and yet we forget. Huh.

SABBATH

The principle of Sabbath is fairly easy to understand: *Don't work.* Pretty much since the very beginning God's people have argued about what "don't work" really means, practically speaking.

Of course, this is particularly challenging for people who are heavily involved with churches. My premise is that since church staff are often ambiguous about how this applies to them, they teach on it even less than they teach teenagers about sexuality.

Our culture generally accepts Sunday as the Sabbath day, even though a more traditional Jewish understanding would be sundown on Friday to sundown on Saturday. But for most church staff, Sunday is their big workday. Everything in the work week leads up to Sunday services. However, for the people coming to church, Sunday is the closest thing they have to a

Sabbath day.

Blah. Blah. Blah. Don't get hung up on the details of "when" to the point that you don't actually embrace the principle of Sabbath in your life. (More on this in a bit.)

AND KEEP IT HOLY...

The last phrase of this commandment is the most important—even more important, I believe, than the *don't work* part.

The idea of keeping it holy simply means demarcating your Sabbath from all other days. On any other day, you can work. But on the Sabbath, you rest. You recreate. Literally, take the word apart and you see the prefix: to Sabbath is to re-create, to create again.

If you don't do anything else on your Sabbath do this: Make it different from every other day.

And when you do? You aren't just setting that day apart, you are also set apart from the rest of society.

Sabbath Is About Trust

We live in the city of San Diego. Our particular area, Mid-City, is extremely diverse culturally, ethnically, and religiously. One group of neighbors who make our area unique is a group of conservative Jewish families that live a few blocks north of us.

When we first moved in I just thought they were hippies. They wear clothes that look homemade. One family has a collection of old Volkswagen camper vans. And several families have turned their front and backyards into giant gardens that produce year-round fruits, vegetables, and even ponds where they raise tilapia.

In fairness, since we live in Southern California, none of this is altogether weird or even sticks out. But the thing that is weird, the thing that demarcates them from everyone else in our community, is their literal observance of Sabbath. In a college neighborhood dominated on Friday nights by young adults going to parties, you'll find these families walking to synagogue or sitting on their front porches playing with their children.

Six days a week they blend in. But one day a week they stick out.

It begs the question: *How do I stick out? What is it about the way I live my life that demarcates me from anyone else? Do I do anything that lets people know I live a life like Jesus' life?*

As I've reflected on my Sabbath-keeping Jewish neighbors I've begun thinking about the Sabbath differently. It isn't just a matter of not working; that cheapens it a little.

Keeping the Sabbath takes preparation. If you're not going to make meals on your Sabbath, you're going to need to prepare for that. If you're not going to use your Sabbath to run errands, you'll need to prepare for that too. If you're not going to work on the Sabbath, you'll need to make sure you get your work done before Sabbath begins.

But ultimately, Sabbath isn't just about not working or about preparation, it's about trust. God is asking us to trust him enough that six days of work will provide seven days of sustenance for your family. And each week he's asking, "Will you trust me in this?"

Who Feeds You, Anyway?

On a Sabbath, while he was going through the grain fields, his disciples plucked and ate some heads of grain, rubbing them in their hands. But some of the Pharisees said, 'Why are you doing what is not lawful to do on the Sabbath?' And Jesus answered them, 'Have you not read what David did when he was hungry, he and those who

*were with him: how he entered the house of God
and took and ate the bread of the Presence, which
is not lawful for any but the priests to eat, and
also gave it to those with him?' And he said to
them, 'The Son of Man is lord of the Sabbath.'*
                                              – Luke 6:1-5

This is one of those passages that I've glossed over
for years. But lately I've been drawn to its intricacies,
which unlocked the bigger picture.

First and foremost, the complaint never made sense
to me until I started reading Mishnah.[5] Various rabbis
orally passed down their interpretations and instruc-
tions on Sabbath regulations from rabbi to rabbi. While
the written Old Testament gave general directions for
obeying the Law, Mishnah was the oral tradition that
defined the specific boundaries. And depending on your
rabbi and who trained him, your oral tradition told you
how many steps you could take on the Sabbath to not
be considered "working."

Alternatively, tradition taught you how to cook in a
way that wasn't work for the cook or work for the
animals who provided sustenance. As referred to in the
passage, there were disagreements among the traditions
about pulling an ox out of a hole to save its life. Was
it OK to do that on the Sabbath or should we wait

until sundown? Was it OK to save a human life on the Sabbath? Or was it better to just save a person's life but not try to heal her any further until after the Sabbath? Various rabbis had various opinions that were passed down through the ages.

Back to the passage above. While all agreed the Law of Moses required farmers to leave a few rows of grain unharvested along the road for the poor or traveling to glean, there was disagreement as to whether it was lawful for people to glean on the Sabbath. So, when Jesus replies back to the Pharisee referring to Old Testament passages, the Pharisees are really trying to figure out which oral tradition gave him permission to glean on the Sabbath.

He frustrates them by offering a remixed version. He didn't respond from the perspective of a certain rabbi. Nor did he respond by quoting the Law of Moses. Instead, he asked a question that reframed the inquiry altogether.

Even if you obey the Sabbath, who is the Lord of the Sabbath? And ultimately, who feeds you from his gleanings: the farmer or the Father?

Physical Food

Think about this for a second: Who feeds you physically? Our food chain is so messed up that I don't think we can possibly comprehend this question. In my fridge right now are fruits and vegetables grown on a farm about 30 miles from where I live. There is also the milk which came from another farm in California. And that cheese? It came from yet another farm in California. Juice? Well, some of the actual fruit came from Australia and the rest came from a chemical plant in Ohio.

The sad reality is that we are so far removed from our sources of food that this passage is completely foreign to us. We don't have a clue who our food actually comes from! Our best guess is that we kind of know the grocery companies that we purchase food from. And we certainly don't go and glean from farmers' fields when we are out of cash or on the road. The farmers might shoot us!

Ultimately, as Jesus points out, God provides the food. As messed up and distorted as our food chain is, God is the ultimate source of food. While I don't think he is the author of high-fructose corn syrup, grain filler, and the other GMO rubbish most of our food is laced with, he is the ultimate provider of both the food that we eat and the money we use to buy it. It all comes from him.

Emotional Food

If we zoom out the lens just a little bit we can ask a deeper question: Are you free to eat emotionally on the Sabbath? Are you disengaging enough to listen? Not just to the preacher or the Sunday school teacher or to other people in your small group. But are you slowing down enough on your Sabbath to hear the voice of the Holy Spirit in your life? Is he feeding you words of instruction, comfort, and rebuke? Or are you drowning the Spirit out by turning the volume up too loud with the human voices in your life?

Are you slowing down enough on the Sabbath to listen to your own voice? Are you taking time to process the stuff that is happening? Are you taking time to rest your body? Are you taking time to rest your mind by doing recreational activities?

That's emotional food. The passage evokes a visual of Jesus and his disciples walking along the road, probably quietly as they observe the Sabbath. The group has spread out, gleaning the grain as they walk—each plucking heads of grain and grinding away the chaff between his fingers or with his palm before popping the uncooked grain into his mouth. This isn't quick, like tossing a bag of popcorn in the microwave! It took time. And it was likely full of introspection and listening.

Who feeds you emotionally during quiet times of self-reflection? Who speaks to you and gives you emotional food to prepare for the week ahead?

Spiritual Food

Finally, we zoom out the lens on this passage as generously as it goes. With our wide-angle lens Jesus asks the question, "Ultimately, who is the Lord of the Sabbath? Who is in charge of the Harvest?"

Jesus is our ultimate source of nutrition. He is the Provider. He gives us life. He made the sun, which warms the soil and provides the energy for photosynthesis.

Spiritually, Jesus is the source of life on the Sabbath. Rather than leaning on the interpretations of man alone—modern-day Mishnah—Jesus is eternal, alive today, and active among his people, bringing nutrition to the poor and sojourners among us willing to glean along the roadside.

Clearly and obviously, Jesus wants us to gather with fellow believers to corporately worship him on the Sabbath. But he doesn't want us to get lost in the granular act of going to church for spiritual food That's a supermarket approach, when Jesus gave us the example of finding food where we are on the Sabbath. He reminds us again and again, "I am the Lord of the Sabbath. It belongs to me. It's ultimately about me. You want to rest, it's found in me. You want to eat, I am the Bread of Life."

Sabbath is a technology which sets us apart as uniquely trusting him. Yes, the world is 24/7/365. But it doesn't mean you need to be connected or engaged all the time. Trust the technology God has provided.

Sabbath and Tuning In

So, what does this have to do with technology—in a more traditional sense—and social media?

Absolutely everything.

If the Sabbath is about trust, then skipping the Sabbath is about power and control.

God says, "I've got you." But most of us say, "I've got me."

Like my own life/work relationship in my early years, it amazes me how few of my friends in ministry have a life outside of their work. There's something deeply broken in our tribe that mistakes working 24/7/365 when the Fifth Commandment asks us to trust God enough to work 24/6/313.

Perhaps the root of it is that we've not taken the time to understand the role recreation can play in our lives. All too often people burn out of ministry. Things stop going well and instead of stepping back to trust, relying on God to sustain them, they forego taking care of themselves and work harder.

I know that in chapter two I argued against retreating from life, particularly as it relates to our lives online.

But let me be clear, what you post online can be a positive or a negative exhibition of your ministry life. One of the biggest surprises happens to me when a Facebook friend or Twitter follower texts me to ask about something I do recreationally on my Sabbath. "What's going on with the Aztecs? Did you catch anything fishing? What are you building in your backyard?" What's most interesting, what sticks out most, what is most remarkable to many of my friends isn't my six-days-per-week ministry—it's my Sabbath.

If you are me, what does that tell you?

Recreate Like Your Life Depends on It

The flip side is also true. You can tell when people don't have a life. Everything they post online is about their ministry. Seven days a week they are posting about being at work, meetings, Bible studies, youth group events, staff events, church services, volunteering in kids ministry, and so on. They are either doing ministry or hyping their ministry. They look exhausted and one-dimensional, probably because they are.

Even when they take days off work they take days off work to read books about work. *Don't do that.* Read fiction on your day off. If it's related to your work it doesn't count as recreation and it's not a Sabbath activity.

Based on what you see posted online, all of their friendships are also tied around their positions at their churches. This means even when they aren't working they are still around work friends or families from church. I know a large number of people who cannot take a day off, much less embrace a lifestyle that includes Sabbath. I once had a mentor who challenged me to develop friendships with people who didn't go to my church and didn't know or care about my position in life, and taking his advice has been one of the most healthy practices of my life. I encourage you to do the same.

People who don't have friends outside of their work lives are people who live on Burnout Boulevard. They are ticking time bombs. I grieve for them. Sadly, we wait for the self-destruction to begin. Which will it be? Their personal life, their ministry life, or their health?

What Does a Sabbath Look Like?

Let's close on a super practical note. Sometimes when I talk about embracing a Sabbath lifestyle, I think some blow it off because it sounds boring. It's not.

Here's what the Sabbath looked like for me one day this summer.

5:00 AM – Alarm
5:30 AM – Drive to Bayside Park in Chula Vista
6:00 – 9:00 AM – Paddle 2.5 miles and fish, completely alone almost a mile offshore in the bay—glassy water, crazy peaceful
10:00 AM – Arrive back home
10:30 AM – Leave for church
11:00 – 12:30 PM – Church with the family, getting church-y
1:00 PM – Lunch at In-n-Out
1:45 – 2:15 PM – Nap!
2:30 PM – Leave for a Mission Bay play day with friends

3:00 – 7:00ish PM – Splashing, kayaking,
   picnicking, and otherwise playing with friends
7:30 PM – Arrive back home, wash down all the
   fishing and boat gear

On that day I watched the sunrise by myself as I paddled in San Diego Bay. I watched the sunset with friends in Mission Bay. A perfect start. A perfect finish. A glorious Sabbath.

Remember, the Sabbath isn't just about not working. Sabbath is practically trusting the Lord to provide seven days of provisions for you and your family in only six days of work. Sabbath is something you do to express your faith in a Provider. Sabbath is an act of worship.

Tuning In Principle:

Tune in to your role online.

CHAPTER 4
The Most Powerful Person Online

In late December 2013 and early January 2014, I responded to hundreds and hundreds of comments on my blog post, "Why You Should Delete Snapchat." More than 500 of these comments were posted directly on the blog post itself. Hundreds more were posted on Twitter and Facebook. To this day—and I suspect for the rest of my life when Snapchat is in the news— people will tag me in their comments about the app to seek my comment.

You know what I've discovered that's crazy? It's atypical for an author to respond to that many comments. It amazes me how many Christian leaders have either completely disabled any option to leave comments or simply ignore them altogether.

I'm sure they have their reasons. But I love that level of

engagement, even (and especially) when it's combative. And it wasn't until the past year or so that I've really started to understand why some people dug in and embraced online discussion, debate, and commenting while others steered clear.

The Power Shift We Feel, But Struggle to Understand

As social media gains traction in our society, we've seen it bend the arc of power in uncomfortable ways. Perhaps nothing better illustrates this quite like the election of Donald Trump. By any traditional understanding, Trump shouldn't have made it out of the primaries. An under-qualified populist, he seemed to take every opportunity available to disqualify himself and none of it worked.

In 2004, Howard Dean was eliminated from the primaries because he had a habit of doing exactly the types of things that Trump eventually rode to the White House doing in 2016. Paul Maslin, one of Dean's chief strategists wrote:

> *He refused to be scripted, to be disciplined, or to discipline himself, in his remarks about every-thing from the Red Sox and the Yankees to Middle Eastern diplomacy. I later likened it all to repeat-*

edly tapping an egg against the edge of a kitchen counter: eventually the egg would break. That's what happened in Iowa.[6]

So, what changed between pre-social media 2004 and social media-driven 2016? The axis of power.

Think about it like this: Let's say you are a pastor, and you are in the pulpit delivering the Sunday morning sermon. By a traditional measure of power you'd be the most powerful person in the room, right? You are on a platform physically and metaphorically above everyone else. Your voice is amplified with a microphone, so that you are louder than everyone else. You are standing (power) while others are seated submissively. Nothing will happen in the room until you are done. Hierarchically, psychologically, ecclesiologically you are the most powerful person in the room.

Right? *Wrong*. Maybe that was the case years ago. But not anymore.

When you are up front, your position is among the weakest in the room because you are the most vulnerable. While you are chained to a (most likely) predetermined script, while you are standing above everyone on the platform, while your words are amplified and recorded, no one else in the room is as bound in that moment as you are.

If you say something interesting, people could pick up
their smartphones and start googling it while you're
speaking. If you're boring, they might start shopping.
If you're controversial, they could start texting. If
you misspeak, there may be a meme posted on your
Facebook profile. And if they disagree with you, they
could subtweet your message to death before you even
know.

See, the power in the room has shifted. What we once
saw as weakness has now morphed into a strength. And
what we traditionally held as powerful is now more
vulnerable than ever.

But why?

Shame.

Trump rose in popularity because he mastered this.
While he stood up front in a position of weakness, he
turned people publicly shaming him into millions of
dollars in free marketing for his campaign.

Many pastors in America are facing an identity
crisis because they are holding on to a 20th century
understanding of power in the 21st century.

Let me explain.

Anthropologists note that social media has largely displaced our 20th-century guilt culture in exchange for a new twist on ancient shame culture.

Christianity Today's Executive Editor Andy Crouch distinguished it like this:

> *The idea of 'shame cultures' originated with anthropologists. During World War II, Columbia University anthropologist Ruth Benedict was trying to make sense of the cultural patterns of the Japanese. Her 1946 book,* The Chrysanthemum and the Sword, *popularized the idea that Japan was a 'shame culture,' in which morality was governed by 'external sanctions for good behavior.' In other words, you know you are good or bad by what your community says about you. By contrast, in a guilt culture such as the West, you know you are good or bad because of an 'internalized conviction of sin'—by how you feel about your behavior and choices.*[7]

Let's use a recent news story to decode the difference between guilt society and shame society.

> *A well-known Tallahassee pastor was forced to*

flee naked after a husband came home early and
found him having sex with the man's wife.[8]

Seems pretty cut and dry, right? There's absolutely no
way this pastor is keeping his job. He wasn't accused
of having an affair. The article details how the woman's
husband *caught* them in the act, retrieved his handgun,
and chased him out of the house while he was still
naked, only relenting after a police standoff. He's
guilty. The jury wouldn't even need to deliberate on that
one. He committed adultery, therefore his consequence
is removal from his post.

In a guilt society this pastor is so obviously fired.

But in a shame society he only bears the consequences
if his community choses to shame him.

> *'I'm hurting because I've hurt you,' Simmons*
> *said January 22. 'I can't speak to people on the*
> *outside. I am not Tallahassee's pastor. I am not*
> *Florida's pastor. I am Jacob Chapel's pastor. It*
> *hurts me that you have to defend my actions. You*
> *cannot defend sin,' he continued to loud applause*
> *from the congregation.*[9]

See, in a shame culture he kept his job as the church's
pastor because his community embraced the idea that

80

his indiscretion (shame event) didn't disqualify him as their pastor. Instead it qualified them to give him (more) honor because he was no better than them in needing forgiveness of his sins.

Crazy, right? I told you power was shifting in uncomfortable ways.

Keep your pants on. I'm leading you towards something here. Trust me.

Attaining Power in This New Paradigm

Let's turn this on its axis one more time. When it comes to life online, people are paralyzed by the fear of shaming events.

David Brooks of the *New York Times* wrote, as a follow-up to Andy Crouch's *Christianity Today* article:

> *Crouch argues that the omnipresence of social media has created a new sort of shame culture. The world of Facebook, Instagram and the rest is a world of constant display and observation. The desire to be embraced and praised by the community is intense. People dread being exiled and condemned. Moral life is not built on the continuum of right and wrong; it's built on the continuum*

of inclusion and exclusion.[10]

They are afraid to be shamed. And most are afraid they'll accidentally shame someone.

This isn't the first time we've found ourselves in a shame society. In Nathaniel Hawthorne's *Scarlet Letter*, readers are drawn into Hester Prynne's nobility when she endures years of public shame as an unwed mother. While—on the other hand—her lover, the Reverend Arthur Dimmesdale, falls into misery as he endures years of *private* shame. When he finally publicly proclaims himself Pearl's father the weight of his shame literally kills him. (Spoiler alert!)

The question facing each of us now is: In today's shame culture, who is the most powerful voice? Is it the enforcers, those who publicly shame others? Or is it the defenders, those who stand between enforcers and those shamed? Or is it those who remain silent, carefully not taking sides for fear of retribution?

This plays out daily on social media. Think of it like a teeter-totter.

Enforcers, adult bullies, spend their days loading up their shame canons to fire at their next victims. Armies of their friends line up to retweet, research, and refine the attack for maximum effect on the victims.

They sit on their end of the teeter-totter with all of their accusations' weight.

Conversely, people pile on in defense to protect their own honor or the honor of their friends.

They put all of their weight on their end until the teeter-totter tips in their direction.

And who wins on the teeter-totter? The one who gets off first.

Interestingly, researchers are studying all of this behavior in the context of school bullying. While lots of attention is paid to understanding the people on the teeter-totter, one study looked into why people don't get involved and remain silent bystanders:

> *As the tendency to feel shame is associated with the need for approval and acceptance… shame-prone students with outsider tendency probably do not intervene in favor of their victimized peers due to their fear of being negatively judged by their peers. Shame might also hinder outsiders from aggressing or from intervening in favor of the victims, because both bullying and defend-*

ing behavior need some extent of dominance and self-efficacy—characteristics that shame-prone individuals often lack... [11]

So, who is the most powerful person online? Easy. The most powerful element of the teeter-totter isn't the people applying weight, it's the thing in the middle. Without the fulcrum you have a plank and you don't have a teeter-totter.

Therefore, the most powerful person on social media is the moderator.

In a shame-based society the moderator is the one who hosts the conversation, who tips the weight of the dialogue back and forth in search of a resolution. The moderator refuses to allow bullies to activate defenders in an endless game of tit-for-tat.

Most importantly, the moderator decides when everyone gets off the teeter-totter, so that everyone leaves with their teeth.

This is what I find so interesting about Christian leaders' typical unwillingness to engage in conversations online. Their silence, their unwillingness to engage, yields an otherwise pastoral role to non-pastoral people. They shift from being the fulcrum, the seat which best represents justice, to being an outsider. To loosely paraphrase a statement from the *Journal of Adolescence*: *Shame-prone Christians with outsider tendency probably do not intervene in favor of their victimized peers due to their fear of being negatively judged by their peers.*[12]

Let's clarify: The moderator is not lacking an opinion or even an implicit agenda. However, the moderator's role does uphold the honor of all perspectives, defend against shaming, and create space for minority opinions and voices to be heard. Good online moderators, people like Rachel Held Evans, acknowledge the humanity of others even when they sternly disagree. (This moderator role may also be why Held Evans has 100,000 followers on Twitter, whereas the average church in America does not.)[13]

In my experience, if you want to develop a powerful voice today, you had better sharpen your skills as a moderator. You must set aside a 20th-century understanding that being neutral means being uninvolved in the daily conversations of your community and instead become willing to enter into the fray, allow yourself to get dirty, give voice to opinions you disagree with, and make sure others honor one another enough in their disagreement to shake hands at the end.

Tuning In Principle:

Tune in to sacred spaces.

CHAPTER 5
I Married Kristen, Not an iPhone

A couple years ago I was having dinner at a Panera in the Boston suburbs. With nothing else on my agenda for the night, I decided I'd observe the relationship patrons had with their phones while they were in the restaurant.

I picked a spot where I could see the dining area. I set up my laptop, so I could take notes. And wore my headphones, so I'd blend in—even though the audio was off. For the next couple hours, as I ate my own dinner, I wrote down dozens of observations, carefully noting what I was seeing and hearing from patrons as it related to their devices and social media.

About 30 minutes after I sat down, a man sat down near me with his son. The man was in his late 30s, tall, handsome, and clearly a professional of some variety. It was the middle of winter, so as he sat down he took off his long scarf and overcoat, then his suit coat, and neatly folded them over the chair next to where he would sit. I imagined that he worked in downtown Boston, probably in finance, as his expensive clothing and attire gave off a vibe that he was comfortable wearing these kinds of clothes. His son looked about six years old, and he followed after his dad, plopping down directly across the table. Before he sat down, he dutifully took off his gloves, hat, and scarf, shoving them in the pockets of his heavy winter jacket before taking it off and stuffing it onto the chair next to him.

As kids of that age are prone to do, the boy talked nonstop. His dad obviously loved every minute of it. While the son got comfortable, fiddling with the Panera pager, I watched as his dad reached into his pocket, discretely pulled out his iPhone, powered it off, and slid it into the pocket of his jacket in the chair next to him.

Soon the pager for their food went off, and the dad went to collect their tray of food. The dad was very caring and made sure his son had everything he needed before he began eating. Over the next 15 minutes or so, the two of them sat there, eating their dinner and having a long, detailed conversation. I surmised from the conversation that the dad didn't live with his son. He asked about all of the highlights of a recent trip his son took with his mom, where they'd gone and what they'd done. As a child of divorce myself, it struck me how respectful the dad was of his former partner. He was careful to be very positive about the trip and everything related to the child's mother. After 25 minutes or so, when dinner was over, the two reversed the process, bundled up, and left.

A few minutes later, at a different table near me, another father sat down with his high school-aged daughter. Technically, she chose the table and sat down several minutes before her dad.

When her dad finally made it to the table, he was talking on the phone. I'd heard this person talking loudly on the phone when he was in line, seemingly oblivious to the fact that others around him could hear his end of the conversation. He wore a flannel shirt and blue jeans and had on one of those big, poofy vests. He also, prominently, had a handsfree Bluetooth earpiece on, which he never took off. If I had to guess, he struck me as a contractor. I envisioned him driving a pickup truck with racks on it for carrying lumber.

Their pager went off, and the daughter got up to get their food while dad took yet another call. Over the next 20 minutes or so, they sat across from one another, only briefly making small talk about their food between calls. The daughter was either staring at her phone or eating. They barely made eye contact.

When they were done eating they got up and left.
I stayed another hour or so, observed a dozen or so
other patrons in all, then called it a night.

Later that evening, with snow falling heavily outside
my hotel window, I spent some time reviewing my
notes. As I thought about the two interactions of dads
with their kids I noted the obvious contrasts in my
notes. One dad was blue collar, one white collar. One
child a boy and the other a girl. One in elementary
school and the other in high school. One intentionally turned off his phone, while the other used his
throughout the meal. One spent a lot of time talking to
his child, while the other didn't.

Lots of things about these two families were different.

But as I spent time thinking through the contrasting
observations I noted one important similarity. Both
dads, when they put the key in the ignition to leave,
likely had the same thought: "I just had dinner with my
kid and that was pretty cool."

Dopamine and the Neuroscience of Attention

Each of us, whether we've ever thought about it or not, now has a relationship with our mobile devices. We likely spend more time with these devices than any human in our lives. We sleep next to them. We keep them in our pockets or purses. We protect them from getting wet and make sure they stay charged. We even take them to the bathroom. They go to work with us, they are in the middle of every conversation, they keep track of where we go, what we buy, how far we walk, on and on. Recently I've noticed that my iPhone even offers me directions to places where it *thinks* I'm likely to want to go.

Mobile devices are inanimate objects, yet we treat them like an intimate partner.

> *...Imagined vibrations as well as people's con-*
> *stant urge to clasp and monitor their phones*
> *are signs of their (research subjects) perceptual*
> *sensitivity to their mobile devices and the impulse*
> *to be tuned in to instantaneous information and*
> *communication access and exchange at all times.*
> *However, this apparent sense of connection with*
> *far flung social and organizational networks and*
> *an outward sense of control over information*

> *flows come at the cost of withdrawal from local and proximal interactions and resentment among in-person friends and colleagues.*[14]

In other words, we have a tendency to divide our attention negatively between an inanimate object (our phones) and the people with whom we should be having real face-to-face interactions.

What's disturbing is that research proves we are fully aware of this, yet we don't do anything to stop it.

> *There seems to be limited denial of one's own tendency to be distracted by mobile devices during face-to-face encounters. Roughly half (50%) of people reported they only rarely pay attention to their cell phone/tablet when talking to a friend in person. Consistent with this, roughly half (52%) of those surveyed reported that female friends routinely ignore them and (43%) reported that their male friends routinely use cell phones during face-to-face encounters. Participants seemed to accurately gauge and acknowledge their distraction during face-to-face encounters.*[15]

So, why is that? Why is our relationship with the mobile phones in our lives so weird?

The truly crazy thing about this falsely intimate, distracting, and destructive relationship with our mobile devices? Most of us never made the rational choice to allow this level of access. These mobile devices crept into our lives over time. We do everything with them and most of it is subconscious.

In 1997, I stood in front of family and friends and vowed allegiance to Kristen. Why is it that 20 years later I'm willing to wait in line, fork over $500, and begin an intimate relationship with an inanimate object that feeds me information I neither need nor want 24 hours per day?

Why is this?

Surely, I'm not alone in repeatedly declaring: "I married my wife not this phone!"

The "why" to that question is as sinister as it is practical. When we think of Silicon Valley we think of Apple, Google, and a whole host of tech startups, we probably imagine their payrolls being dominated by software engineers.

And this is true to a certain extent.

What most of us don't think about is how much physiological and neurological manipulation goes into app and device design.

> *Mixpanel, a mobile analytics company, created a report called Addiction that looks at how often people use an app throughout the day. The company's report (which frames app addiction as a positive trend, given the revenues this behavior generates for app makers) suggests that social apps take the cake for addiction. In 2014, 50 percent of social users spent at least five hours per day social networking, and the top 20 percent spent upwards of eight hours daily. Some users checked social apps every waking hour of the day. Messaging apps were found to be less addictive than social apps, and media apps were the least addictive.*
>
> *'Your ideal customers are the people who engage with your product at least once every day—better still if they're using it constantly,' the Mixpanel report asserts. And that's certainly the accepted sentiment in the tech community.[16]*

How did this happen?

When smartphones took off in popularity between 2007 and 2009, people started to notice that users carried over the same looping behavior that they did on their desktop computers, just more frequently because the device was with them more often.

Here's what I mean. Most users have a loop of behaviors that they do out of habit. Clinically, it's referred to as a compulsion. Here's how a 2012 article in *The Atlantic* explained the phenomenon:

> ...*Before long, people were referring to their BlackBerries as CrackBerries, and parents were beginning to worry about the number of hours their kids spent on video games. We now believe that the compulsion to continually check email, stock prices, and sporting scores on smartphones is driven in some cases by dopamine releases that occur in anticipation of receiving good news. Indeed, we have grown so addicted to our smartphones that we now experience 'phantom smartphone buzzing,' which tricks our brains into thinking our phone is vibrating when it isn't.*
>
> *By the time Web 2.0 rolled around, the key to success was to create obsessions. Internet gaming companies now openly discuss compulsion loops that directly result in obsessions, and the goal of other applications is the same: to create the compulsion to gather thousands of friends on*

Facebook, thousands of followers on Twitter, or be pleasantly surprised to discover from Foursquare that a friend you haven't seen for years is nearby.[17]

For me, my loop (i.e., compulsion) looks like this: First I check my email, then I look at Twitter, followed by Facebook, then I look at Instagram. Each time my workflow is interrupted or I'm momentarily bored I check this loop. Your loop might look different from mine, but we all have a loop. And every developer is trying to figure out how to get you to add their app to your loop. This addictive behavior has been understood for a long time, and most users experience it to one degree or another.

But then came the rise of texting. What we learned is that because of the perceived intimacy of a text message, receiving a new text message interrupted everything and consequently actually restarts the compulsive loop.[18]

Many studies have shown that users might check their loop every 15-20 minutes throughout the day out of habit, but if they receive a new text message the average user will check that message within five seconds.[19]

Unlike the loop, which is a learned habit or compulsion, this newfound ability to interrupt the loop or anything else you were doing—from an important meeting to having sex—sent developers in a whole new direction. What they discovered was that the notification of a text message, the buzz or beat that your phone made, triggered a dopamine-fueled response. In other words, once you were conditioned to believe the interruption might be something important or good, your brain's reward system was on alert for these types of rewards.

As a result of this discovery, app developers started building in new ways to trigger that response.

> *Internal triggers rely upon associations in the user's mind to prompt actions. The most frequent internal triggers are emotions. When we're feeling lonely, we check Facebook. When we're uncertain, we Google. When we're bored, we watch YouTube videos, check Reddit or scroll Pinterest.*
>
> *Habit-forming products align the external trigger (a push notification, for example) with the moment when the internal trigger is felt (say the feeling of uncertainty or boredom). The closer the timing of the external trigger is with the internal trigger, the sooner the association is formed.[20]*

Suddenly, device manufacturers realized they could impact your behaviors at the subconscious level if they gave app developers access to trigger this dopamine at the right time. This gave birth to the notification. If an app sends a push notification or an audio alert, you will check that app whether it's actually important or not because your brain's reward system has been activated. This is why apps want you to turn on push notifications that buzz, ding, or otherwise interrupt you. They are attempting to make using their service more and more compulsive. This is also why I advise everyone I know to disable as many notifications as they possibly can.

So, why do you have an intimate relationship with your phone, one which may actually be impeding your relationships with the most important people in your life? Some of it is your fault; you've developed bad habits. But some of it is the design of the devices themselves. They are using the latest neurological research to trigger compulsive reactions for their own profit.

Don't even get me started on Candy Crush.[21]

Creating Sacred Spaces

Our mobile devices have invaded family life. When I share the story above about two dads with parent groups and school groups, I get two very different responses.

Parent groups recognize that they want to be the first dad, though they feel guilty because they are most likely the second dad. It's a powerful allegory, as they each want to be the person who turns off his phone to have a great conversation with his child over dinner.

But student groups? *Sometimes they applaud.* For them, when I share this story, it's the first time that an adult in their lives gets it from their perspective. While these devices have crept into the lives of adults, they've always been there for most of the youth. Most of their parents have had mobile phones their entire lives. And, now that the smartphone has the power to interrupt everything, children typically resent their parents' relationships with phones. They wish they had the power to interrupt that a push notification has.

I believe each family needs to create sacred spaces where mobile devices are forbidden. This isn't retreating from the interaction that social media brings, it's setting apart times and places where you are beyond the reach of your device, where you can invest in face-to-face meaningful conversation with the people who matter most to you without the temptation to answer a text message or peek at a notification.

Much like fasting, the discipline of maintaining sacred spaces is incredibly freeing, as is the reality that you aren't all that important—that it's OK to be unreachable or disconnected—and that you own your device, it does not own you.

In our house, the dinner table is our sacred, internet-free space.

When we moved from Michigan to San Diego in 2008, we left our dining room table behind. And until about 2014, we didn't have a dinner table. Our house was small and it just didn't seem worth the space.

But, especially for Kristen, meal time had become a pain point. She'd spend tons of time making delicious, healthy meals, and when it was time to eat everyone would come grab a plate and disappear in front of the TV or a computer. Consequently, we were rarely all sitting in the same place. This strained every relationship in the house.

And so, problem solvers that we are, we went out and bought a dining room table. Upon bringing it home, Paul, our middle child, declared: "That's the stupidest thing you've ever brought into this house."

We put the table together, and from that point on we

have had five or six meals together each week. And you know what? Everyone looks forward to dinner time, even Paul.

Yes, meal-making and cleanup is still a chore. But for a moment every day the five of us sit down together without distraction. We talk about our days. The boys usually say or do something to gross out everyone else. We eat. We joke. Nothing magical happens there, no one leads a family devotion or anything like that. We just eat a meal together. And you know what? It's become the most healthy thing we do as a family.

The lowly dining room table is the best technology we've ever purchased for our family. (Sorry, Apple.)

One of the incredible things we've learned about creating a sacred space in our family is that our kids look forward to it; they need it. What's hilarious is that they are disappointed when I suggest that we just grab a plate of pizza and plop down in front of the TV.

See, the table isn't just sacred to mom and dad. It's sacred to the whole family.

In your house it doesn't have to be a dinner table. But each household would be wise to create and protect specific places and spaces where the internet doesn't reach. We need to have Twitter-free zones or places where no one is going to Snap a picture to a friend.

Lastly, I believe, this does need to be sacred. Set it apart from everything else you do. It needs to be special, it needs to be something you fight for, and it needs to be something everyone accepts and honors.

Fostering Sacred Routines

I don't want to paint our family as having it together when it comes to technology. But we have stumbled on a couple of things we've found helpful.

As I've already mentioned, the dinner table has become a sacred routine. But we've also established a few other routines, which help remind us that while we are a highly internet-connected family, we own our devices instead of the other way around.

DO SOMETHING ON SUNDAY

As we've taken Sabbath more seriously, including limiting church activities on Sunday to worship services only, we've established a pretty solid routine of doing something together on that day each week. Most often, this involves us going to the beach or bay. But sometimes it's something less exciting like doing yardwork together or cleaning the house. The point isn't that we're doing something spectacular as a family, the point is that we're doing something that separates us from our normal routine of being online all the time.

EVENING WALKS

Again, this isn't magical, but most evenings Kristen and I walk the dogs. Sometimes we "splurge" by taking the dogs to a dog beach, but most often we just put leashes on them and walk for a couple of miles. What's great about this routine is that it's pretty easy to forget about your device.

VACATIONS

I'm a huge fan of using every last ounce of vacation time I can muster. And while vacation time is often scattered throughout the year, we have one large, coordinated family vacation that we look forward to each year. For the past several years, we'll have two parts to our vacation. The first part is camping in Yosemite National Park, and this is device free. The second half is usually staying at a resort or renting a beach house where we allow everyone to do whatever they want with their devices.

Again, honoring something as sacred means that it's different—set apart—from everything else you do. Yes, there are other times we go to the beach or walk the dogs or even go on trips. But we have specific routines built into our family life that are sacred, internet-free zones.

Repeat after me: *I own the device, the device does not own me.*

Tuning In Principle:
Tune in to thriving.

CHAPTER 6

Thriving Is Success

All you need in life is ignorance and confidence,
and then success is sure.

— Mark Twain

Imagine you wake up tomorrow morning to a
messenger banging at your door who informs you that
a long lost relative you've never heard of has died
and named you in the will as the sole recipient of his
massive estate.

After a few days of paperwork you find yourself with
enough money in the bank that you'll never need to
work again for a paycheck, never have to think about
money, you'll never even have to see what a checkbook
or bank statement looks like again, because you'll have
a staff of people who take care of that kind of thing for
you.

Now, six months go by.

You've long since stopped showing up to the job you have today. You've bought all the cars, planes, houses, and boats you could think of. You had Adele sing "Happy Birthday" at your birthday party. You've flown in Denzel for dinner. You've given away embarrassingly large sums of money.

So, now you have a problem. *You're only 25 years old.* You've got at least 50 years of living left, and you need some sort of purpose for your day-to-day life beyond swimming in the life-sized reproduction of Scrooge McDuck's swimming pool.

With all of your material needs met, what are you going to do?

Since the pursuit of money is now off of the table, what are you going to define as success?

> What will occupy your time?
> What will keep you busy?
> What will be your career?
> What will challenge you?
> What will get you out of bed in the morning and
>   bring you joy during the day?

For me, I think there are some aspects of working at The Youth Cartel that I'd continue doing. But there's a

110

whole lot of stuff that's "just work" that I'd never think twice about leaving behind. (Inventory, accounting—stuff like that.) If someone were to show up at my door tomorrow and take care of all of the needs of my family for the rest of my life, we'd upgrade where we live, probably including some islands and homes in our favorite places. And I'd certainly spend a whole lot more of my time fishing, playing golf, and investing in entrepreneurs.

But what else would I do to occupy my time? What else would bring purpose? How would I define success in that scenario?

Why does this matter?

I find this exercise useful because it helps you get to the heart of the matter: *What is it that I should be doing?* It's a fair and legitimate thing to mix up your definition of a successful life with providing for your family.

> *Success is relative. It is what we can make of the mess we have made of things.*
> – T. S. Eliot

December 28th, 2013, began a period that most people would perceive as professional success. Judging by the sheer volume of teasing from my friends, this is hard to argue with. By most external measures, it was a great success.

- As of this writing, that blog post has been read more than four million times.
- The ad revenue on that was lovely. (Thank you, Google Ads.)
- Hundreds of thousands of people were alerted to problems with an app they trusted, helping to prevent exploitation.
- While not directly related, the Federal Trade Commission and Snapchat reached an agreement to deal with the problems I addressed in the blog post.
- I spent the next year speaking at dozens of schools, churches, and community groups about internet safety.
- I sold lots of books, did lots of radio and television interviews, and have been quoted in lots of magazines, newspapers, and other places.

And yet, as I shared in chapter one, in hindsight I don't view what happened as a total success.

If there's been a long-term success as the result of what happened, it's been that that period of my life provided me with an opportunity to reevaluate what I was going to define as successful.

I spent 111 days on the road in 2014. I made more money in 2014 than I'd ever made in a single year. And I did things in 2014 I'd never thought possible.

While I enjoyed all of those opportunities I was given—especially to speak to so many middle and high schoolers around the country—at the end of 2014, I found myself more exhausted than I'd ever been. I was buried in work, struggling with the existential question "Who am I and what is 'this' all about?"

Whatever it was, it didn't feel like success. And looking forward to the next 25 years of my career, I needed to reevaluate what kind of success I was looking for.

What Is Success When You Can Work 24/7/365 and No One Cares?

This isn't just an Adam question. This is a question all of us face.

- What is "it" for us?
- What is "enough" for us?
- What is "the goal" for us?

Here's a dirty little secret about being self-employed that you've probably never heard about: *No one cares.*

At some point, whatever you do for work, you'll do it well enough that only you will care or know if you're successful in the ways you are measuring.

Here are some things that allowed me to reconsider and reorient.

In *A Parent's Guide to Understanding Social Media*, which I wrote with Mark Oestreicher, a central theme for me was the relational goal I have for my kids, that they will grow up to develop happy, healthy, and simple adult relationships.

And when I cowrote *Good News in the Neighborhood*, Jon Huckins and I helped youth groups realize the importance of knowing your neighbors well enough to serve them, to be the hands and feet of Jesus.

But what about me? Could I really travel 111 days per year and still help my own kids develop into adults who have happy, healthy, and simple adult relationships? Heck, could I have happy, healthy, and simple adult relationships? Could I travel 111 days per year and legitimately know my neighbors well enough to be the hands and feet of Jesus to them?

114

Of course not. So, I either had to live a hypocritical life—given the things I'd written (and things others expected of me)—or I'd need to change. I decided to change. I limited my travel, I reordered my schedule so I could spend more time one-on-one with my kids, I built an office at home and stopped renting an office in another part of town, and I found a few ways to get involved in my community.

Again, if I expect the people in my life to hear Good News then my life better be Good News. Ultimately, people want to know, "Does a life with Jesus work?" And if they see in you a workaholic whose life is a mess, then what they know about Jesus is that he's not working for you. *So why bother exploring a life with Jesus for themselves?*

The sad reality is that technology gives each of us the "opportunity" to work all of the time, and no one will look down on us, no one will think better or worse of us for doing so. Particularly if we're in ministry, no one seems to push back when we work 50, 60, 70 hours. Instead, we see it as a noble sacrifice when, in fact, that's not honoring to us or our ministries in any practical way.

Reorienting Success

Like anyone who has been in vocational ministry for a while, I know far more people who have washed out than I do people who have stuck it out.

As an idealistic 18-year-old, I set out to live a life in youth ministry. And as an idealistic 40-year-old, that's still my goal.

Success isn't about numbers. It's not about money. For me, a successful life and ministry comes from doing the right things for a long time in a sustainable way. No one wants to be a one-hit wonder. I don't, you don't.

What we want to be is Steve Fisher.

Casual college basketball fans will know Steve Fisher as the Michigan coach who recruited the Fab Five, who led them to the Final Four, and who was later fired when it was discovered that Chris Webber had been receiving impermissible benefits from a booster.

And, sadly, this is how things work in our society. We tend to think of people singularly. If we know one thing about Steve Fisher, it's that he was fired from Michigan. But that was really only the beginning of what's become an incredible story at San Diego State University. Coach Fisher arrived on campus as the head basketball coach in 1999. His arrival on campus wasn't celebrated nationally. San Diego State had never been any good at basketball so why should anyone take notice?

Yet, since then, Steve Fisher has built something truly remarkable. He and his staff have slowly built a perennial powerhouse program in San Diego. Coach Fisher once distributed tickets on campus for free to try to persuade people to come to games, whereas now their arena has sold out every one of their 12,414 seats for six seasons in a row and counting.

Currently in his 70s, Coach Fisher's legacy has long since moved on, past his failures at Michigan. Now, in the coaching world, Steve Fisher is known as the man who built a program where there wasn't one before.[22]

When we reorient success beyond the one-hit-wonder and instead strive for something which will endure long after we're gone, we will value things like loyalty, ongoing improvement, the hard work of true evaluation, a posture of coachability, the process of healthy critique, and the building up of people around us.

When I think about success, I no longer think about myself exclusively. I judge the success of my ministry

117

by what I can help develop in others, who will then exhibit our shared values. It's not about me, ultimately, my individual life is part of something bigger. That's success.

Thriving As Your Ministry

"A healthy ministry flows out of a healthy you." Some variety of this mantra has floated around in youth ministry circles for as long as I can remember.

The problem is that most of us don't know what healthy looks like, but we have loads of examples of people who *aren't* healthy.

In this book, I've tried to point toward some of the practices I've added into my life, which exhibit health and which have unleashed something like thriving in my life. That doesn't mean I'm a model of health, but the idea is to point toward things that establish healthy habits.

Pretty regularly, I hear questions from churches about how to fairly pay their youth workers. I understand the struggle. Each church wants to make sure that their person is paid the market rate—that's fair, right? But they also want to make sure they aren't breaking their own budget or stretching too far financially to support the ministry. Over the past couple of years I've been challenging these churches to not think about the cost of *living* in their community but instead to calculate the cost of *thriving* in their community. Over and over again I encounter friends in ministry who just aren't making it financially at their churches, but they aren't off by much. A few hundred extra dollars per month would be the difference between them sweating the bills and enjoying the occasional movie date with their respective spouses. That inability to thrive financially causes an incredible amount of stress, which sadly means that they develop unhealthy habits. Because when people feel as though they lack control in one area of their lives, they often overcompensate by hyper-control in another.

I believe the same thing is true as we calculate our vocational lives. All too often we worry about doing enough to justify our positions or salaries. And, trust me, this leads far too many into unhealthy habits, where they work all the time and never seem to take care of themselves. The consequences are a life that isn't thriving, isn't successful, and is ultimately not a vocational life worth living.

Instead we should reorient our lives—from the priorities we value to the way we spend our off days to the technologies we use—to be about thriving.

Success is like a garden. It's the result of doing the right things for a long time.

Finally, my challenge is not to pursue thriving as simply a way to model healthy living for someone else. My challenge is to pursue a thriving life which wildly and selflessly follows Jesus wherever he may lead, because that's ultimately why we entered into this life to begin with.

Endnotes

1. You can see one of our selfies from the top of the mountain here: https://www.instagram.com/p/iZ2bGsMjvB/.

2. This insightful Gutenberg quote can be found online here: http://www.beliefnet.com/quotes/evangelical/j/johannes-gutenberg/yes-it-is-a-press-certainly-but-a-press-from-wh.aspx#Sx5Q281AcgwCLDDR.99.

3. Adolar Zumkeller, *Augustine's Rule: A Commentary*, translated by Matthew J. O'Connell, edited by John E. Rotelle (Villanova, PA: 1987). For online version, see: http://midwestaugustinians.org/roots-of-augustinian-spirituality/.

4. You can learn more about the Ignatius Examen here: http://www.ignatianspirituality.com.

5. You can learn more about Mishnah here: https://en.wikipedia.org/wiki/Mishnah.

6. Paul Maslin, "The Front-Runner's Fall," *The Atlantic*, May 2004, https://www.theatlantic.com/magazine/archive/2004/05/the-front-runner-s-fall/302944/.

7. Andy Crouch, "The Return of Shame," *Christianity Today* (print and online), March 10, 2015, Vol. 59, No. 2, pp. 32: http://www.christianitytoday.com/ct/2015/march/andy-crouch-gospel-in-age-of-public-shame.html.

8. Ryan Dailey, "Fla. Pastor Flees Naked and Afraid, Begs Forgiveness for Tryst," *USA Today Network* (online), source: Tallahassee Democrat, January 30, 2017: http://www.usatoday.com/story/news/nation-now/2017/01/30/fla-pastor-begs-forgiveness-tryst-after-being-caught-naked/97263088/.

9. Ibid.

10. David Brooks, "The Shame Culture," *The New York Times*, March 15, 2016: https://www.nytimes.com/2016/03/15/opinion/the-shame-culture. html?_r=0.

11. Angela Mazzone, Marina Camodeca, Christina Salmivalli, "Stability and Change of Outsider Behavior in School Bullying: The Role of Shame and Guilt in a Longitudinal Perspective" *The Journal of Early Adolescence*, July 22, 2016: http://journals.sagepub.com/doi/pdf/10.1177/0272431616659560.

12. Ibid.

13. These numbers were accessed from https://twitter.com/rachelheldevans in January 2017.

14. Shalini Misra, Lulu Cheng, Jamie Genevie and Miao Yuan, "The iPhone Effect: The Quality of In-Person Social Interactions in the Presence of Mobile Devices," *Environment and Behavior* (online), July 1, 2014: http://journals.sagepub.com/doi/abs/10.1177/0013916514539755.

15. Catherine Chambliss, Emily Short, Joshua Hopkins-DeSantis, Heather Putnam, Brittany Martin, Megan Millington, Allison Frymoyer, Gena Rodriguez, Lacey Evangelista, James Newman, Amy Hartl, and Jennifer Lee , "Young Adults' Experience of Mobile Device Disruption of Proximate Relationships," *International Journal of Virtual Worlds and Human Computer Interaction*, Vol. 3, 2015: https://www.researchgate.net/ profile/Catherine_Chambliss/publication/272398337_Young_Adults'_ Experience_of_Mobile_Device_Disruption_of_Proximate_Relationships/ links/5616511708ae73279641cc55.pdf.

16. Felice Miller Gabriel, "App Makers: It's Time to Stop Exploiting User Addiction and Get Ethical," *VentureBeat* (website), April 2, 2016: http://venturebeat.com/2016/04/02/app-makers-its-time-to-stop-exploiting-user-addiction-and-get-ethical/.

17. Bill Davidow, "Exploiting the Neuroscience of Internet Addiction," *The Atlantic* (online), July 18, 2012: https://www.theatlantic.com/health/archive/2012/07/exploiting-the-neuroscience-of-internet-addiction/259820/.

18. Britney M. Wardecker, William J. Chopik, Margaret P. Boyer, Robin S. Edelstein, "Individual Differences in Attachment Are Associated with Usage and Perceived Intimacy of Different Communication Media," *Computers in Human Behavior* (journal), University of Michigan, June 2016, Vol. 59, p. 18-27: http://edelsteinlab.psych.lsa.umich.edu/pubs/Wardecker%20et%20al%20CHB%202016.pdf.

19. "Text Message Marketing: The New Kid on the Block," *SlickText* (online), February 13, 2014: http://www.slicktext.com/blog/2014/02/text-message-marketing-the-new-kid-on-the-block-infographic/.

20. Ximena Vengoechea and Nir Eyal, "The Psychology of Notifications," *TechCrunch* (online), February 5, 2015: https://techcrunch.com/2015/02/05/the-psychology-of-notifications/.

21. Maria Evangeline Varonis, "Deconstructing Candy Crush: What Instructional Design Can Learn from Game Design," *The International Journal of Information and Learning Technology*, Vol. 32, Issue 3, p.150-164: http://www.emeraldinsight.com/doi/abs/10.1108/IJILT-09-2014-0019.

22. You can learn more about Coach Fisher here: http://www.goaztecs.com/sports/m-baskbl/bio-Fisher.html.